# Garfield at large

BY: JIM DAVIS

BALLANTINE BOOKS · NEW YORK

All rights reserved under International and Pan-American Copyright
Conventions. Published in the United States by Ballantine Books,
a division of Random House, Inc., New York, and simultaneously in Canada
by Random House of Canada Limited, Toronto, Canada.

Library of Congress Catalog Card Number: 79-93191
ISBN 0-345-32013-1

Manufactured in the United States of America

First Edition: March 1980

50   49   48

PURRR

I HATE STATIC ELECTRICITY.

7-3 JIM DAVIS

I REALLY SHOULDN'T EAT THAT FISH...

7-4

© 1978 United Feature Syndicate, Inc. JIM DAVIS

CALL IT AN ETHNIC WEAKNESS.

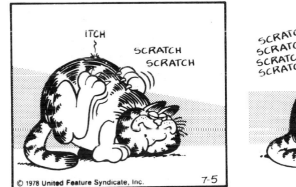

AH, A CURTAIN UPON WHICH TO SHARPEN MY CLAWS.

© 1978 United Feature Syndicate, Inc. 7-7

I HATE DOUBLE-KNIT.

JIM DAVIS

DEAR GARFIELD: BELIEVE IT OR NOT, I AM AN UGLY KITTEN! OH, I DO ALL THE THINGS "CUTE" KITTENS DO...PLAY WITH YARN AND SUCH, BUT I DON'T GET ANY ATTENTION. WHAT CAN I DO?

MUD FENCE

DEAR "MUD": YOU'RE TRYING TOO HARD TO BE CUTE. YOU'LL GET MORE ATTENTION IF YOU JUST BE YOURSELF...

7-8

AND SHARPEN YOUR CLAWS ON THE LIVING ROOM DRAPES.

JIM DAVIS © 1978 United Feature Syndicate, Inc.

LOVE A COOKOUT

MIND IF I SMOKE?

© 1978 United Feature Syndicate, Inc.

JIM DAVIS

I'M GOING TO TAKE AN ACTIVE PART IN ENERGY CONSERVATION.

7-13

GET ON YOUR MARK, GET SET...

© 1978 United Feature Syndicate, Inc.

CONSERVE

JIM DAVIS

AH, HERE COMES THE MAIL MAN.

7-19

WHY SHOULD DOGS HAVE ALL THE FUN?

JIM DAVIS

OH BOY, OH BOY. TODAY IS THURSDAY, AND THAT'S LASAGNA DAY.

7-20

CAT FOOD!

GARFIELD

GARFIELD

JIM DAVIS

7/23

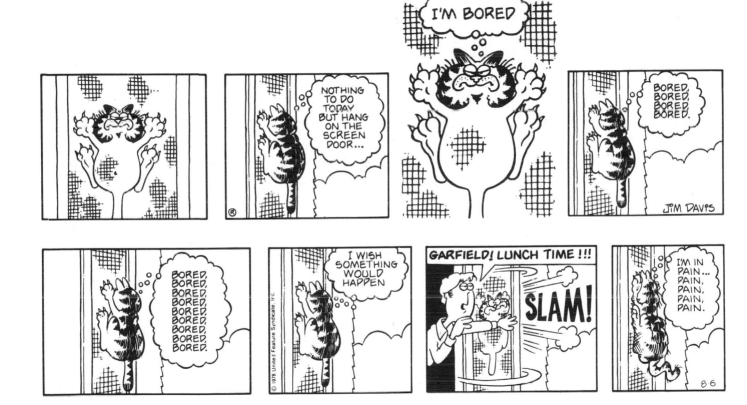

8-25

© 1978 United Feature Syndicate, Inc.

JIM DAVIS

© 1978 United Feature Syndicate, Inc.

SPLOOCH!

8-26

HELP YOURSELF TO THE LASAGNA, GARFIELD.

JIM DAVIS

GARFIELD, AS OF THIS MINUTE, I'M PUTTING YOU ON A DIET

8-28 © 1978 United Feature Syndicate, Inc.

GARFIELD?

I THINK I SNAPPED HIS MIND

JIM DAVIS

COME ON, OLD BUDDY. GOING ON A DIET'S NOT ALL THAT BAD. WHY, A COUPLE OF POUNDS OFF THE MIDDLE AND YOU'LL BE FIT AND TRIM AGAIN

8-29 © 1978 United Feature Syndicate, Inc.

THAT'S BETTER

JIM DAVIS

I DIDN'T HAVE THE HEART TO TELL HIM HE'S MADE THE WEIGHT WATCHER'S TEN MOST-WANTED LIST

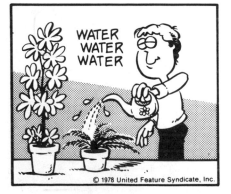

10-16

I THINK I'LL HAVE GARFIELD DECLAWED

© 1978 United Feature Syndicate, Inc.

JIM DAVIS

GARFIELD, I'M GOING TO HAVE YOU DECLAWED

10-17

TAKE AN ARM! TAKE A LEG! BUT SPARE MY CLAWS!

YOU'RE GOING TO BE DECLAWED AND THAT'S THAT. NOW GET YOUR HEAD OUT OF THE OVEN!

JIM DAVIS    © 1978 United Feature Syndicate, Inc.

© 1978 United Feature Syndicate, Inc.

© 1978 United Feature Syndicate, Inc.